Road Atlas

★

Also by Campbell McGrath

Road
Atlas

*

Prose & Other Poems

by CAMPBELL MCGRATH

THE ECCO PRESS

THE ECCO PRESS
100 West Broad Street
Hopewell, New Jersey 08525

Published simultaneously in Canada by
Publishers Group West Inc., Toronto, Canada
Printed in the United States of America

Library of Congress Cataloging-in-Publication Data

McGrath, Campbell, 1962–
    Road atlas : prose & other poems / Campbell
        McGrath. — 1st ed.
        p.   cm.
    ISBN 0-88001-668-X
    I. Title.
    PS3563.C3658R63   1999
    811'.54—dc21   98-37078
                                                    CIP

9 8 7 6 5 4 3 2

FIRST EDITION 1999

For Sam & Jackson

✦

For Elizabeth

✦

For James Wright

Acknowledgments

With thanks to the editors of the following publications in which some of these poems originally appeared:

Harvard Review: "Albergo Santa Restituta"
Indiana Review: "Baker, California," "Four Clouds Like the Irish in Memory," "Rice & Beans"
Kenyon Review: "A Dove," "Capitalist Poem #42," "Port Olry"
Luna: "Las Vegas," "Mountainair, New Mexico"
Mangrove: "Jimmy Buffett"
Ohio Review: "Sylvia Plath"
Paris Review: "Plums," "The Prose Poem"
Ploughshares: "El Balserito," "Praia dos Orixas," "The Wreck"
Quarterly West: "The Gulf"
Sycamore Review: "A Map of Dodge County, Wisconsin"
TriQuarterly: "Biscayne Boulevard," "Dinosaurs"

Several of these poems were published in *Mangrovia*, a limited edition chapbook, from Short Line Editions, St. Paul, MN.

Grateful acknowledgment is made to the FIU Foundation and to Kingsley and Kate Frost Tufts for grant money which enabled this book to be completed in a timely fashion.

Contents

★

*What thoughts
can I call allies?*

—SAM SHEPARD, *MOTEL CHRONICLES*

Road Atlas

The Prose Poem

On the map it is precise and rectilinear as a chessboard, though driving past you would hardly notice it, this boundary line or ragged margin, a shallow swale that cups a simple trickle of water, less rill than rivulet, more gully than dell, a tangled ditch grown up throughout with a fearsome assortment of wildflowers and bracken. There is no fence, though here and there a weathered post asserts a former claim, strands of fallen wire taken by the dust. To the left a cornfield carries into the distance, dips and rises to the blue sky, a rolling plain of green and healthy plants aligned in close order, row upon row upon row. To the right, a field of wheat, a field of hay, young grasses breaking the soil, filling their allotted land with the rich, slow-waving spectacle of their grain. As for the farmers, they are, for the most part, indistinguishable: here the tractor is red, there yellow; here a pair of dirty hands, there a pair of dirty hands. They are cultivators of the soil. They grow crops by pattern, by acre, by foresight, by habit. What corn is to one, wheat is to the other, and though to some eyes the similarities outweigh the differences it would be as unthinkable for the second to commence planting corn as for the first to switch over to wheat. What happens in the gully between them is no concern of theirs, they say, so long as the plough stays out, the weeds stay in the ditch where they belong, though anyone would notice the wind-sewn cornstalks poking up their shaggy ears like young lovers run off into the bushes, and the kinship of these wild grasses with those the farmer cultivates is too obvious to mention, sage and dun-colored stalks hanging their noble heads, hoarding exotic burrs and seeds, and yet it is neither corn nor wheat that truly flourishes there, nor some jackalopian hybrid of the two. What grows in that place is possessed of a beauty all its own, ramshackle and unexpected, even in winter, when the wind hangs icicles from the skeletons of briars and small tracks cross the snow in search of forgotten grain; in the spring the little trickle of water swells to welcome frogs and minnows, a muskrat, a family of turtles, nesting doves in the verdant grass; in summer it is a thoroughfare for raccoons and opossums, field mice, swallows and black birds, migrating egrets, a passing fox; in autumn the geese avoid its abundance, seeking out windrows of toppled stalks, fatter grain more quickly discerned, more easily digested. Of those that travel the local road, few pay that fertile hollow any mind, even those with an eye for what blossoms, vetch and timothy, early forsythia, the fatted calf in the fallow field, the rabbit running for cover, the hawk's descent from the lightning-struck tree. You've passed this way yourself many times, and can tell me, if you would, do the formal fields end where the valley begins, or does everything that surrounds us emerge from its embrace?

Plums

I'm sitting on a hill in Nebraska, in morning sunlight, looking out across the valley of the Platte River. My car is parked far below, in the lot behind the rest stop wigwam, beyond which runs the highway. Beyond the highway: stitch-marks of the railroad; the sandy channels and bars of the Platte, a slow wide bend of cottonwood saplings metallic in the sun; beyond the river a hazy, Cezanne-like geometry of earthy blues, greens, and browns fading, at last, into the distance. Barrel music rises up from the traffic on I-80, strings of long-haul truckers rolling west, rolling east, the great age of the automobile burning down before my eyes, a thing of colossal beauty and thoughtlessness. For lunch, in a paper bag: three ripe plums and a cold piece of chicken. It is not yet noon. My senses are alive to the warmth of the sun, the smell of the blood of the grass, the euphoria of the journey, the taste of fruit, fresh plums, succulent and juicy, especially the plums.

So much depends upon the image: chickens, asphodel, a numeral, a seashell;

one white peony flanged with crimson;

a chunk of black ore carried up from the heart of anthracite to be found by a child alongside the tracks like the token vestige of a former life—what is it? *coal*—a touchstone polished by age and handling, so familiar as to be a kind of fetish, a rabbit's foot worn down to bone, a talisman possessed of an entirely personal, associative, magical significance.

Why do I still carry it, that moment in Nebraska?

Was it the first time I'd been west, first time driving across the country? Was it the promise of open space, the joy of setting out, the unmistakable goodness of the land and the people, the first hint of connection with the deep wagon-ruts of the dream, the living tissue through which the valley of the Platte has channeled the Mormons and the 49ers, the Pawnee and the Union Pacific, this ribbon of highway beneath a sky alive with the smoke of our transit, the body of the past consumed by the engine of our perpetual restlessness? How am I to choose among these things? Who am I to speak for that younger vision of myself, atop a hill in Nebraska, bathed in morning light? I was there. I bore witness to that moment. I heard it pass, touched it, tasted its mysterious essence. I bear it with me even now, an amulet smooth as a fleshless fruit stone.

Plums.

I have stolen your image, William Carlos Williams. Forgive me. They were delicious, so sweet and so cold.

Baker, California

How many times through the suburbs of loneliness, isolated galaxies of vitriol and salt? How many times this transfigured iconography, the dry hum of terror and desolate generation? Trona, Kelso, Baker, how many journeys unto the gates of Death Valley? How many nights without refuge before one is forever marked and transformed? If the desert burns it is a property of darkness, windspur and cloven hoof, thistle like the portal of violet resolve. If the night reveals its inner self it is a property of vision, a kind of violent light, sheer and lapidary, gas stations, restaurants, assembled legions of last chance motels, nothing-ness amid the nothingness of everything and nothing. *Ultraviolet* is the world I'm looking for. The *word*. It is the word I'm looking for. The moment, the place, the power and righteousness of a certain melody, not even needing to believe its dark intransi-gence but hear and glory in it only, the moment when noise begins to resemble music, when music comes to resemble noise. This journey, that journey, burdens and joys as hallucinatory as heat waves, the past a mirage of irredeemable distance, the place where light crosses over to water, where water reduces to light. How many times such transubstantiation? Angel of chaparral, angel of mercury vapor, how even to talk about those days now?

Years later, Elizabeth and I came upon it like a vision in the wilderness, checked in to the same room at Arnie's Royal Hawaiian, the same tepid shower, the same beer and pretzels from the Stop N Go store. It was late, pitch black for hundreds of miles, and lovely in the false blue light of palm trees and neon, the rich green glow of the swimming pool. Try as I might, there was nothing I could say or do to convince her how terrible this place was, how abject a seat of desolation, why it signified despair and the madness despair brings down like unearthly snow. On TV, black and white helicopters circled the latest disasters: a train wreck, a toxic spill, a forest fire raging out of control in some wild scrub hills outside of—outside of Baker, comes a voice above the buzz of copter blades, the whole town of Baker could be at risk, is all we hear, before the audio sheers to static. Once, in New York, I saw two planes collide in midair: walking along the dock at 79th Street, deep indigo Hudson River dusk, suddenly looking up to a ball of flame, a blur, objects tumbling along divergent arcs like dancing partners slipping their moorings; the first crashing in flames atop the palisades, starting up small ruby tongues that dozens of fire engines struggled to control over the next three hours; while the second vanished beyond the heights, a palpable concussion as it hit and exploded amongst oil tanks miles away in New Jersey. I saw this, and I tell you, that moment in Baker was stranger. In room 106, all is still but the air conditioner. Beyond the window: night, blue palm trees, nothing. On TV: images of flame, multitudes of flame, silent minions and consorts of flame. We move outside to the parking lot and stare into the impervious darkness. Nothing. The ice machine whispers erotic riddles, the edge of something almost cool passes over us in the breeze. Nothing. When we come to the pool we take off our clothes, part the brilliant water, immerse our bodies in its radiance until they transform to fluid emeralds.

Baker, California, is not hell, though it bears a family resemblance. That night was no infernal mime, though it carries still a tinge of the otherworldly. The forest fire burned in Baker, Oregon, a place I'd never heard of, absurdly far away, and by morning the fire-fighters had brought it under control. Exhausted, we slept late, and when we opened the door the dry heat sucked the night's memory from our lungs. The sun was a hammer that bent our bones like iron bars in a forge. Heat-shimmers hissed audibly as they rose in swells to fuse with the roar of traffic and vanish in the colorless vacancy of the sky. Song of the oven of days. Song of the soul in the furnace of the body. At our feet, the desert begins. The grass gives out, the parking lot peters into dust, the endless grey ruined skin of the world runs off into eternity. And there is nothing I can say or do to help you.

Yogurt & Clementines

Dinner at a small restaurant I have happened upon by chance
after a long day walking the city of Tunis, a neighborhood place
among passageways of date palms, clean and friendly, where I
am catered to like a meteorite crash-landed in the courtyard.
Cracked grains and parsley, tuna fish, coarse bread. Salad of
chopped and spicy peppers. And then dessert, and suddenly
everything is washed away — dust of the Sahara upon my tongue,
odor of sour clove at the heart of the medina, the alienation of
foreign currency, the sorrow of the alley cats among the ruins of
Carthage, its weird light and fragmented crypts, headless torsos,
fields sewn with salt, exile and loss, even my harrowing
loneliness redeemed by a saucer of sweet and liquid yogurt,
golden clementines from a branch freshly cut, stems and leaves
still attached, an inchworm marking the course of his dinner,
gratefully, undisturbed, mouthful by tiny mouthful.

Praia dos Orixas

for Robert Hass

1

Farther north we came to a place of white sand and coconut palms, a tumbledown government research station, seemingly abandoned, no one in sight but sea turtles lolled in holding tanks along the edge of the beach. The ocean was rough, riptides beyond a shelf of underlying rock, water a deep equatorial green. We swam. Rested. Hid from the sun in the shade of the palms. A few miles on we found the fishing village by the inlet, the small restaurant with platters of squid and giant prawns on a terrace overlooking the harbor, manioc, sweet plantains, beans and rice in the lee of the cork-bobbed nets and the tiny cerulean and blood-orange fishing boats sheltered in the crook of the breakwater's elbow. A boy selling sugarcane rode past on a donkey; white-turbaned women bent like egrets to the salt marsh. "There is no word for this in English," said Elizabeth,

meaning, by *this*, everything.

Later: goats and dogs on barbed-wire tethers; children laughing beneath banana leaf umbrellas;

women hanging laundry on a red dirt hillside in a stately ballet with the wind.

2

The next day we headed back to the city, following the rutted dirt road along the coast until forced to a halt with the engine of our rented Volkswagen thumping and billowing a fatal tornado of smoke.

Fan belt, snapped in two.

It was difficult making ourselves understood in that place; they seemed to speak some backwoods dialect, or else the language failed us completely; neither Anna's schoolbook Portuguese nor JB's iffy *favela* slang brought any clear response. People beneath strange trees ignored us in the darkness, or watched with an air of unhappy distrust, or disdain, or possibly compassion.

Although we couldn't see the beach, a sign by the road read *Praia dos Orixas.*

Eventually, one man took pity upon us, running home and returning with a fine black fan belt fresh in its package, a fan belt big enough for a tractor, impossible to jury-rig to that clockwork machine, and yet no matter how we contrived to explain ourselves, no matter what gesticulations we employed, what shadow play, what pantomime, we could not make him see that his gift would not suffice. *No good! Too big!* We held the broken belt against his, to display their comic disparity, but the man only smiled and nodded more eagerly, urged us to our task of fitting the new piece, happy to be of assistance, uncomprehending. *Won't fit! Too big! Thank you, friend!*

Hopeless.

In the end, money was our undoing, those vivid and ethereal Brazilian bills stamped with the figures of undiscovered butterflies and Amazonian hydroelectric dams. I forget whose idea it was to pay the man for his kindness, but no sooner had the cash appeared in our hands than he at last gave vent to his anger and frustration, insulted by our mistaken generosity, hurling epithets that needed no translation, and so, as the crowd approached, menacingly, from the shadows, or perhaps merely curious, or possibly protective,

we jumped in the car, still smiling, waving our arms like visiting dignitaries, desperate to display the depths of our goodwill but unwilling to risk the cost of further miscommunication,

and drove away with a gut-wrenching racket into the chartless and invincible night.

3

What follows is untranslatable: the power of the darkness at the center of the jungle; cries of parrots mistaken for monkeys; the car giving up the ghost some miles down the road; a crowd of men with machetes and submachine guns materializing from the bush, turning out to be guards from a luxury resort less than a mile away; our arrival at Club Med; the rapidity of our eviction; our hike to the *fazenda* on the grounds of the old mango plantation where we smoked cigars and waited for a ride; the fisherman who transported us home with a truckload of lobsters bound for market.

By then another day had passed.

It was evening when we came upon the lights of the city like pearls unwound along the Atlantic, dark ferries crossing the bay, the patio at the Van Gogh restaurant where we talked over cold beer for uncounted hours. That night was the festival of São João, and the streets snaked with samba dancers and the dazzling music of *Trios Elektrikos*, smell of roasting corn and peanuts, fresh oranges, fire crackers, sweet *ginepapo*, veins of gold on the hillsides above the city where flames ran shoeless in the fields among the shanties, warm ash sifting down upon our table, tiny pyres assembled around seashell ashtrays and empty bottles as the poor rained down their fury upon the rich. That night the smoke spelled out the characters of secret words and shadows were the marrow in the ribs of the dark. That night the stars fell down,

or perhaps it was another.

That night we yielded to the moon like migrating sea turtles given over to the tide-pull.

That night we clung together in the heat until dawn as the cries of the revelers ferried us beyond language.

That night we spoke in tears, in touches, in tongues.

Port Olry

Here the gods came down from the hills and paused at the edge
 of the sea.
Here they rested, wrapped in grass, speaking together as the
 mountains speak, tongues clacking like the beaks of
 ancestral storks,
and looked back at the undulant jungle, ridges and river
 valleys, islands scattered like shark's teeth on a tablet of
 raddled fronds,
and gazed ahead toward the volcanic shadows of even darker
 archipelagoes
where they had yet to sow their baskets of orchids and taro, to
 spin their vindictive spider webs of mist,
those brooding, short-limbed, Melanesian gods, Rain and
 Loam, Centipede and Boar, Root and Yam and Fever.
They squatted on the beach, and wiped their small mouths, and
 shaded their eyes, and saw how it was,
strings of passing squalls above the reef's blue crescent, storm-
 light lustred by rain and passed back, water to water,
flashing in the shallows like the great blue fish the light of the
 sun once was in an amber lagoon at the edge of an
 inviolable ocean.
Heart-sick, weary of jungle, here the gods halted on their way to
 New Guinea.
They saw how it was, and relented, and passed on.

Dinosaurs

Though damaged in the typhoon, the little restaurant came highly recommended. It was tucked away on the outskirts of town, across the lagoon, hard to find among the unfamiliar streets of thatched houses and bungalows, old Quonset huts, the Tonkin-Chinese overseas stores, dim windows of floral fabrics, canned meat, fishing line, hooks and sinkers. The owner, also cook, head-waiter, and busboy for the evening, was a grey-haired Polynesian émigré, a charming man who traveled amongst the few small tables in a comical cowboy hat, bantering and telling jokes, goaded by friends into performing songs of his own composition on the ukulele. The restaurant was famous for flying fox, the giant fruit bat that was a particular delicacy on the island, but with each passing season they were becoming harder to procure, and there were none that evening. Elizabeth ordered the coconut crab; I the cockles in mustard sauce, a Tahitian salad of raw fish and mango in coconut milk. After some wine, the food arrived; Elizabeth's crab was gargantuan, monstrous, prehistoric. The owner showed her how to crack the mammoth claws, fed her forkfuls of steamed white meat tasting of the coconuts the wild crabs subsist upon in their remaining out-island enclaves. A cat appeared and picked at the discarded carapace in a bucket on the floor. It jumped up on the table, upset the flowers, and fled. By the naked fluorescent light above us a gecko, lunging suddenly, seized a giant moth in its jaws and held it, pinioned, as slowly, from the shadowed corners of the ceiling, a dozen lizards converged on the immense, fluttering body, and began, silently, voraciously, to eat. Late as it was, the owner offered to drive us home himself, there were no taxis at that hour, it was his pleasure, his duty, the other diners would pay on their honor if he did not return before they left. He pressed another glass of Armagnac upon us, a vestige of the former French colonial presence; good coffee, grown locally, a new industry for the islands. Deep night had fallen upon the black waters of the lagoon. From the ceiling a fine dry snow fell upon us, the velvet furze of the moth's writhing body and the papery dust of its wings.

2   ENGLEWOOD BEACH, FLORIDA

The fishermen look bored in their totemic t-shirts as they cast and retrieve and cast again into the gulf: Gators, Seminoles, Hurricanes, Dolphins. At the sound of an outboard motor starting up, the great blue heron that dogs them for minnows lumbers with saurian grace to take flight, circles slowly, glides back to the sand twenty yards removed. Underfoot, colonies of coquinas filter the swash zone, a sandy rainbow of rose and lemon and bruise-colored pebbles, the smooth black tridents of petrified shark's teeth. Where seashells are piled in yard-wide drifts, the tide-break, retreating, carries a musical susurrus, like piles of coins raked together, as the slurry of broken shells hisses and jingles and keens and shrills, the chink of slugs for the ocean's ossified silver dollar slot. At the base of an eroded seawall, three poles bound with yellow tape mark the spot where a sea turtle came ashore last night to make her nest. This time of year, volunteers scour the beach each morning for drag marks emerging from the surf, though even when a turtle makes it ashore there is no guarantee it will build a nest, and most of what eggs are laid will be scavenged by raccoons or ghost crabs, and if the lights of the condominiums are not turned off the hatchlings will head inland, across the dunes of morning glory and poverty grass, to perish among deck chairs at sunrise. Pelicans skim the milky water, five and six in a squadron, scattering the terns and sheerwaters from their reveries. Toil of the waves, slow rolling breakers curling at the sand bar, fifty yards out. A plane appears, headed south. The osprey alights in a casuarina. A stingray has washed up on the sand and children are stabbing its body with sticks.

Rice & Beans

"Dad?" Yes. "You are a wimp." That's very nice, thank you. Eat your grilled cheese. "I say you are a *little* wimp. I learn that at school. From a *big* kid." Of course. "Tyrannosaurus Rex, King of the Dinosaurs!" Sam is not yet three. When he roars I stick a spoonful of rice and beans into his mouth. "Dad, did Rex eat ricey-beans?" I think so. "No! He was a *meat* eater." That's right. "They *think* he was a meat eater." Who? "*Scientists*. Dad?" Yes. "Does beans have bones?" No. "Do cheese have bones?" No. "Why do they change the name of *bronto*saurus to *apato*saurus?" I honestly don't know. "*Scientists* know. They know, Dad." Yes. Probably. Drink some water, please. "Dad, water does not have bones." True. "Water does not have hands." Right. "Usually, dogs have no hands. But Scooby Doo have hands. Why, Dad?" He's not a real dog. "Did he *die out*?" He's just a cartoon dog. "Do Scooby Doo eat ricey-beans—*cartoon* ricey-beans?" No. Yes. Probably. I think so. Eat your sandwich. "Dad, I no call you little wimp before. *Rex* call you little wimp." That's not a nice thing to call someone, is it? "Rex is not nice. Rex *mean!*" Sam roars and I stick a crust of sandwich in his mouth. "Dad, can I have a cookie? Vanilla cookie? *Please.*" You haven't finished your grilled cheese, have you? "That's just the bones, Dad. *Toast* bones."

El Balserito

Because my Spanish is chips-and-salsa simple, and I am desirous
of improving upon it, and delighted whenever I can puzzle out
on my own some new word or phrase, I am listening in on the
conversation of the two Cuban men next to me at the counter of
the plumbing supply store in Little Haiti, and when I hear the
word *balserito* I recognize this to be a diminutive of *balsero,* "the
rafter," that symbol of the Cuban-American experience, those
cast ashore on scrapwood rafts emblematic of an entire
community's exile, and when the one man goes out to his truck
and comes back with a little plastic dashboard toy of Goofy and
another Disney character floating in an inner tube, and the
other man, laughing and smiling at the joke asks, *Quien es el
otro?,* pointing at the smaller figure, I know that this is Max,
Goofy's son, because we have just taken Sam to see *A Goofy
Movie,* a story of father-son bonding in the cartoon universe, a
universe in many ways more familiar to me than this one, though
of course I say nothing to the men, not wanting to admit I have
been eavesdropping, or betray my linguistic insufficiency, the
degree to which I am an outsider here, in Miami, a place unlike
any other I have known, a city we have fixed upon like Rust Belt
refugees eager to buy a little piece of the sunshine, to mortgage a
corner of the American Dream, where already Sam has begun to
master the local customs, youngest and most flexible, first to
make landfall, betraying the generational nature of
acculturation the way the poems of my students at the state
university do, caught between past and present worlds,
transplanted parents looking back to Havana while the children
are native grown, rooted to the soil, though the roots of *las
palmas* are notoriously shallow, hence their propensity to topple
in a hurricane, tropical storm, even the steady winter tradewind

bearing its flotilla of makeshift sails across the Straits of Florida, so many this season that some mornings, jogging along the boardwalk in the shadow of the luxury hotels, I have come upon three rafts washed up in a single mile of beach, ragged planks and styrofoam and chicken-wire, filthy and abandoned but curiously empowered, endowed with a violent, residual energy, like shotgun casings in a field of corn stubble or the ruptured jelly of turtle eggs among mangroves, chrysalides discarded as the cost of the journey, shells of arrival, shells of departure.

The Gulf

Floating in the gulf, on a hot June day, listening to the seashells sing.

Eyes open I watch their migrations, their seismic shifts and tidal seizures, as I am seized and lifted, lulled and hushed and serenaded. Eyes closed, I drift amid their resonant sibilance, soft hiss and crackle in the tide wash, ubiquitous underwater, a buzz like static, or static electricity—but not mechanical—organic and musical, metallic as casino muzak, piles of change raked together, a handful of pennies down a child's slide. Eyes open I see them rise as one with the water, climbing the ridge with the incoming surge and then, released, called back, slide slowly down the face of their calcified escarpment, the sandy berm the small rippling waves butt up against and topple over—flop, whoosh—a fine wash of shells and shell bits and shards, a slurry of coquinas and scallops and sunrays, coral chunks, tubes and frills, the volute whorls of eroded whelks, a mass of flinty chips and nacreous wafers, singing as it descends. Like mermaids, singing. But not a song. Stranger and more varied, more richly textured, many-timbred, Gregorian hymns or aboriginal chanting, the music of pygmies in a forest clearing, complex, symphonic, indecipherable. But not human. Elemental. Like rain. Bands of tropical rain approaching from the jungle, sweeping the tile verandah, the sheet metal roof, against the slats of the louvered window and across the floor of storm light and coffee-flavored dust—but not liquid—mineral—mountains of shattered porcelain, broken bottles en route to the furnace—but not glass and not rain and not even a rain of glass. Ice. The day after the ice storm, when the sun peeks out, and wind comes off the lake, and what has so beautifully jeweled the trees all morning breaks loose in a sequence of tumbling cascades, chiming like tumbrels and lost castanets, falling upon snow-covered cars and encrusted fences, discarded Christmas trees piled up in the alley, smelling of wet balsam, string and plastic in their hair, and forgotten tinsel, and every needle encased in a fine translucent sheath of ice, and as I reach to touch them my fingers brush the sand and my knees bump the bottom and I am called back with a start, alien, suspended, wholly conceived within that other music, body in the water like the water in the flesh and the liquid in the crystal and the crystal in the snowflake and the mind within the body like the branch within its skin of ice.

Eyes open. Eyes closed.

Floating in the gulf, listening to seashells, thinking of the Christmas trees in the back-alleys of Chicago.

A Dove

If May is the month of the mockingbird, September is the season of the dove. On the roof they have gathered to drink from warm puddles of yesterday's rainwater, preening and cooing in the shade, while their brothers the pigeons line the telephone wires in radiant sunshine, waiting for their daily feed to spill forth from Mr. Johnson's sack of seed and cracked corn. Sunday morning, 10 a.m. High African clouds in the west, alamanda spilled in yellow spikes and coils across the fence. In the backyard: a neighbor's cat. At the sound of the opening window it flees, startled, then hesitates at the top of the wall to glance back—at what?—and as my eye tracks its gaze I catch a sudden motion in the overgrown grass, frantic circling too big for a lizard, too desperate, and even as I notice it and begin to speak, even as I call out *Hey, come see something strange in the yard* I realize, in that instant, what it must be—a bird, mauled, its weary struggle for survival—and wish I could unsay it, wish I could avert the gaze of my conscience because already I foresee the morning slipping away—a box, a warm towel, a bowl of water, and the calls to the Humane Society, and the drive to Fort Lauderdale to tender its fragile body to the Wild Animal Hospital, a shaded compound of blackbirds and parrots, box turtles and one-eared rabbits—and now Sam has come over to watch with me and I cannot will away the obvious, and he dashes out the back door to investigate, and now the day has been taken from us, seized, wrenched away, a day of rest I would covet even against that ring of blood and spilled feathers, the slender broken bones in the lawn, and now we are drawn into the circle of its small life, obligated by our witness, impossible to deny or retract, committed long before the dull slow course of a thought can be born into language, before the image is set into words, as Sam's words come to me now across the hot summer grass: *Dad, it's alive. A kind of bird. It's hurt. A dove.*

Sylvia Plath

In truth I care little about your mother or your father, scars or bell jars, the suicidal hive, the husband against whom I am ignorantly prejudiced and willing to remain so. It is not the life but the poems that matter to me, those you abandoned with mere hints and allegations, Christmas toys agog on the rug, their hungry mouths, demanding as tulips, impatient as an infant. So they appear, sometimes, as glassy ornaments in a pitch-black elm tree eked from the seeds of predawn misery, the terror of isolation and mist from which they emerged, one a day, as with Van Gogh at Saint Rémy, invoking the torment of root and marrow, touched by the sugar of abandonment, the prefiguration of the void, odor of gas, a new deep bruise, your magic moon in eclipse at last, stiff as a hard-bitten biscuit or British upper lip.

And then the leap, the pall of heaven, ruddy blood, an open oven.

1963. London.

This morning, painting the new bookshelves in the garage, white slabs ready for the wall's empty rack, I watched the sawn lumber rise up as plinths, as teeth in the mouth of one who calls me, as I too am summoned, in the hours before the dawn, by poems and by children.

It is not for your death but for your orphans that I love you.

They are as beautiful as ivory, as adamant as the chisel that carved them. I can see them stretched out before me in the fog

like white stones, mile markers along a country road that ends,
too suddenly, in the last ripe realization of the abyss.

*Totem. Child. Paralytic. Gigolo. Mystic. Kindness. Words.
Contusion. Balloons. Edge.*

Biscayne Boulevard

Crossing the bay: pelicans and buzzards against a Japanese
screen of rifted clouds, squalls and riffs in grey, white, azure.

Color of lead, color of moonlight, color of shallow water.

*

Road crew planting oleander;
two years since the hurricane.

*

The grease monkeys at the gas station on the causeway must
have the most beautiful view of any workers in America.

As a function of growth, life is, thereby, a process of loss.

How the carefree palms who cast their coconuts aside in today's
high wind must feel: strong, unburdened, immeasurably sad.

*

Gulls like asterisks; anhinga like bullets.

*

Sunlight, white hulls, black
cloisters of the mangrove:

such moments I see this world
as it truly is/is not.

*

At 123rd Street: survival
of the fittest franchisee.

Boston Chicken, Pollo Tropical,
Kenny Rogers' Roasters,
KFC.

Which must perish so that another may live?

*

Oceans of Notions.
I.N.S.
The Pussycat Theater.

*

Evenings, working girls from the topless clubs shop their wares
among these stripmalls of chop suey and gospel Creole,

glass bones of liquor stores,

the glorious ruin of these motels: New Deal, Mardi Gras,
Vagabond, Hacienda;

Sinbad, Starburst, South Pacific, 7 Seas.

*

If I were to die
this minute,

now,

I would be with Elizabeth and Sam again

in another world, a world
I do not and cannot believe in.

I know this in the roots of my teeth,
in the lunar plains of my palms.

*

What you call an asterisk I call a bullet.
What you call a bullet I call ellipses.
What you call ellipses I call the eclipse.

*

The bite of the bullet is the mouth-mark of the moon.

The young men running numbers and dust upon the boulevard
conspire in their trade with the aces and deuces of unforeseeable
fortune.

Cop killer. Rhino killer. Black widow. Liquid heart.

*

The bullet, the bullet, the bullet.

*

If I could raise this city into the heavens,
caress it like a polished calabash maracca,
shake it like a shoebox to jar the lucid gunmen
and wingéd cockroaches into the sunlight,
if I could take it in my hands and carry it,

would I?

My compassion is ripe but sour
as the fruit of the lemon tree;

my fear so immediate
it could bring the bay to a boil. Anger
is the mask it wears
like a liquid silver sun
upon these wide but shallow waters,

silent reflection above the dogfish and stingrays,
the weed-eaten chassis of our mutual need.

★

Leopard ray. Mantra ray. Devil ray. Skate.

★

Police helicopter, sweet damselfly, can you track my happiness?
Radar gun, will you enumerate my sorrows?
Bullet, do you sting?

Amsterdam

1

For every life we lead, how many pass unlived? For every future foreseen, how many unimagined? For every turn intended, how many taken wrong, overlooked, stumbled past by accident amid the trumpets and shadows of circumstantial traffic? When my plane landed in Luxembourg, Mike was there to meet me. He was catching the next flight out, his rental car was parked outside, would I take it, please, just have it back in Paris in a week? As usual, Mike was rushed to the point of incoherence. He'd spent the last few days with a famous retired American businessman at his chateau in the Loire, where Mike had shown up uninvited to present his latest improbable money-making scheme, a plan so gigantic, megalomaniacal, and grotesquely unlikely that the famous executive had taken an immediate liking to it, and to Mike, who'd had the audacity to climb the castle walls when turned away at the gate, and thrust himself upon the man out weeding his begonias, and so was invited to stay the weekend, watch horse races on TV with a visiting Duke and Duchess, and sent off with the names of high-level contacts in New York. This explains Mike's rush to get back, despite our loose plans for traveling together. And this explains my presence in Rotterdam, alone, past midnight, driving again and again through the Benelux tunnel, looking for the road to Amsterdam. I had no map, and so I navigated by a schematic outline of Holland on the back of an airline brochure, a strange game of connect the dots—Dordrecht, Leiden, den Haag—points of inconceivably ancient interest drawn together by the random wire of my motion. I had no clear idea where Amsterdam was, nor even why I was going there, only that I couldn't stop now for fear of losing my momentum. And so three times through the Benelux tunnel, three times around that unlovely hub, and then a branching off at random across the countryside, peaceful lights of towns in the satin blackness, past Utrecht and picking up signs again, closing in now, into the suburbs and golden rings of Amsterdam, steering by feel into its ever-narrowing funnel, a place I'd never been, nothing I'd ever heard of and a language I did not know, deeper and deeper into the concentric labyrinth until, shivering with exhaustion, I parked as best I could at the foot of a bridge, climbed the Himalayan staircase of an over-priced hotel, crashed, and slept. In the morning: sound of trucks, horns, commerce. Light through the attic windows and a green diagonal of canal. Streetsweepers in orange bibs, mechanical rotors scouring the cobbles, such tidiness, such order, the car, of course, long since towed away. . . .

2

The authorities wanted over a hundred dollars for the car, so I left it in the police lot and spent the morning at the Van Gogh museum. I checked out of the pricey hotel and into a student hostel, where the semipermanent inhabitants were smoking hash and watching *Green Acres* on the pirate satellite channel. The pace began to quicken. Days, I wandered the streets, sat in the museums, studied Van Gogh. Evenings, I took up with a knife-wielding Hawaiian called Thor, beer-mug washer at a place off the Prinsengracht, where he held court playing high-speed mumblety-peg with bloody-knuckled challengers on the steel-topped bar, which every night at closing he doused with kerosene and danced a flaming war dance atop to the multilingual approval of the patrons. My last night there I met a woman who, in the forthright Dutch manner, asked me back to her houseboat, and in the morning invited me to stay awhile, stay the month, the season, dressed in wool to ward off the smoky winds of winter. This she indicated with her knitting needles, sitting up in bed at dawn, flaxen haired, measuring me for a sweater. What could I say—that I had things to do, obligations, other lives to lead? That Mike's car was still in the pound, due back in Paris tomorrow? How much of this am I imagining and how much is imagining me? That houseboat, the poems I would write there, the tides, the coal barges, the epic investigations, painting the cabin with tiger stripes and crosses, mornings in the fog lugging barrels of diesel fuel for the generator, eros, Rembrandt, the abortion, the eviction, the trip to the Frisian Islands where her father met us at the ferry, salt water and roses, the will of the body written in blood and gin and semen across the dark night of the city, a lock of hair, skeins of wool, canvas, oil, flour, a painting of a man in a rusty sweater absorbed in his writing on the deck of a houseboat as dawn comes through the steeples and chimneys of Amsterdam. The zodiac, the ether, the crystal spheres sometimes align themselves so that there exists for a moment a portal into another reality, a door into another of the silent houses of existence. Several times I have seen that passage, hurried past heedless, without hesitation; twice, three times, I have found the courage to open it, to stand on the threshold and watch, but never to cross over. One step, one footfall, and then—. But there are obligations, considerations. Such tidiness, such order! I do not mourn for the mansion of the past, already in flames as we travel its fugitive corridors, glorious and derelict, wreathed in lucent smoke. Let it burn. Let its ashes configure the constellations of memory, let its embers reside like dwarf stars in the night. Galaxies of darkness, galaxies of light. . . .

Albergo Santa Restituta

It is the premier hotel elected by Ancient Romans as a privileged health resort since VII century b.c. It is built in Roman style and received baroque additions in the XVIII century and the walls have frescoes dating from the school of Giotto of the XIV century in the crypta with the chapels of the noble families. Enjoy the sites where solitude is a choice and meeting is easy and discover the foreshortening of the nature always present for the aperitif or just for a talk. Sites where you meet again with your own harmony in a pleasant dialogue or in the silence of a magic view, so the choice of being in two becomes a nice new discovery. And each day expose oneself to the sun beams, savor the fruit of the best Mediterranean gastronomy whose bright colors blend with flavours you will never forget in a joyful meeting who captures your fantasy, too. Furthermore, terraces overlooking the sea where breeze pleasantly reliefs in the hottest days and brinish spreads its odors elating those who breathe, having their breakfast admiring this intense and pied view. Silent relaxing rooms with precious beds, and flax sheets accurately folded by gentle hands, real wood mattresses inviting to sleep. It seems as if for magic time had stopped here, and walking around its huge halls decorated with exquisite majolicas which still today accompany their guests in a delightful journey, unique in their alternance of hues, you can almost feel the presence of past creatures, full of emotions and sensations, walking down stairs where other people had been walking, along memories of a past kept alive with its strong suggestive-ness. It is equipped with structures for water-sports, squash, solarium, and sauna. It fell into ruin under the British cannons in 1809. It is a place of pilgrimage for people who expect perfection.

Mountainair, New Mexico

Stopped for lunch after crossing the Malpais, that awful wasteland, desolate, sun-stricken, palpably grievous. Eyeless window sockets in the town of Claunch; the ruined pueblo at Gran Quivíra. At the next table folks were talking about the unusual cold of the previous winter, so much snow a bear had come down from the mountains and roamed around town for days seeking shelter. "You remember that bear?" *Oh yeah, yeah. It was living over by Dale's place.* Lunch arrived—egg salad, pickles, iced tea. The door of the diner swung open and a man in spurs and chaps and stetson hat strode in, knocked the dust from his britches, sidled up to the old wooden bar and ordered a glass of milk. It came, full and frothy. The cowboy drank it, wiped his lips on his sleeve, paid, and left. At the next table they were still going at it. "Whatever happened to that bear?" *Dale shot it.* "He shot it? Killed it?" *Yep.* "Is that legal—killing a bear?" *I don't know, but he sure did shoot it.*

Hunger

1

This is a true story. One day when I lived in Manhattan, burglars broke into my apartment and stole my tape deck, my raincoat, and my Incredible Hulk piggybank. I was having a party that night; Bruce and Mike and I had trudged all the way down from 116th Street lugging cases of Genessee beer, bottles of bourbon and tequila, sacks of ice, but as soon as we opened the door I knew.

So.

Briefly, we cursed the perpetrators; we put the beer on ice and discovered the loss of the raincoat, an inexplicable theft; we called the police, who were too busy to trouble with us. And that was it. All in all, Bruce and Mike took it harder than I did, though it had nothing really to do with them. My main concern was this: now we would have to find another tape deck for the party. Beyond that, I was strangely unconcerned. It was only *things*, after all, part of the shell game of material possessions, albeit vital possessions, my tape deck being my primary source of entertainment in those days, music my constant companion, whatever songs obsessed me that week played over and over in a kind of religious-ecstatic frenzy. But Crazy Eddie was full of new tape decks—Crazy Eddie was solvent back then—and the two hundred bucks it would cost was an inconvenient but not impossible loss to sustain. I was working at the 79th Street boat basin as a carpenter, dockhand, watchman; my dad was helping pay for graduate school; student loans took care of the rest. If the banks were unaware I was spending their borrowed money on tape decks and tequila, what fault was that of mine? If I was unaware how long the albatross of debt would hang from my neck, what fault was that of the banks?

2

As to the culprit, I had my suspicions: George, the superintendent, a notorious drunk with a passkey, to whom I'd given a fifth of vodka at Christmas and perhaps this was my thanks in return; Mona, the "model" who lived above me, whose hands-on sagas of needy desperation rung more than a few false notes; the scabrous crackheads living in a broken-down van around the corner, a jacked-up, fire-streaked vehicle we called the Mobile Crime Lab—drugs, guns, what didn't they sell out the back of that van? Whoever they were, the burglars had come and gone by the window. Halfway down the fire escape is where we found the Hulk, abandoned in midheist, a green plastic figurine stamped out by the millions at some factory in China, icon of a frugality beyond my needs or practice, a dead weight of dozens of pounds of pennies.

3

At the party we got drunk and listened to loud music on a walkman jury-rigged through my speakers. A famous poet stood on the bed and left dirty footprints all over my pillow. In the morning I slept late, tidied up, feeling hung over and world weary. In the afternoon I went to work, carried lumber, hammered nails out along the seawall on the Hudson, sat in the little guard shack come evening, buzzing people through the security gate, excluding those who did not belong, until the late-shift guy arrived at midnight, a lovely, heavily-armed Nigerian named Afaso. What I did next speaks volumes: I went home. I was hungry, had eaten nothing since breakfast, but I was also broke, having blown it all on the party, two dollars in my pocket until payday.

Now wait: certainly I could have put my hand on some money with a phone call, borrow whatever I needed from friends, easily, as a matter of course. But I was taking a kind of Spartan pleasure in my poverty that day, my straitened circumstances indulged as a badge of honor, a penance for my losses,

and so I walked the thirty blocks home, fell into bed, and dreamt

that my skin was the color of money.

Everything was backwards: I was stiff with rage when I was supposed to be calm;

I was Lou Ferrigno, but I was supposed to be Bill Bixby.

At the edge of consciousness I could see him, my alter ego, hard at work, typing up scientific formulae, sitting at my desk, in my apartment, but I could not get to him, could not transform back into that version of myself.

My will blew in the wind like shredded paper, a swirling confetti of dollar bills.

I smoked a cigarette and lit fire to my poems. A woman came through the window and put them out while I watched. I paid her money. I slept with her. I was hungry. I was helpless.

I woke near tears.

4

Though it was ten years ago, that dream was one of the most vivid of my life, and I remember it plainly. This year, for the first time, I've started to make money in a reasonable way, a "professional" way. I'm a husband, a father, an assistant professor at the state university. I drive to work in a red station wagon along boulevards of shoe stores and fast food restaurants like any other citizen, like the Joe Taxpayer I have become, a transition from student days that seems profound but really isn't. I'm still in debt, still paying off the borrowed leisure of those apprentice years, but I have never seriously lacked for anything material in my life: in times of relative poverty, I have lived happily poorer; in relative wealth, much the same. Those days on 105th Street I was no more than an interloper, a transient passing through to another life. For all that it was a testament to my buried fears and desires, the secret currency of power and helplessness, bright coins in dark waters, I can see, looking back, that the dream of the Incredible Hulk had little even to do with me, with my life as it would develop, a Polaroid taking on shape and color, rising and brightening away from those mean streets. It was for those from whose shoulders the burdens would not be so easily lifted, those whose deprivation was more than a caprice: for Afaso, the night watchman, in the quiet hours before dawn; for George, the super, drunk again in the basement when the boiler needs fixing; for the junkies, the gypsy cabbies, the street-corner boys in front of the bodega; for those who would steal pennies in their desperation, who violated the sanctity of my small world, who came back three weeks later to take the stereo tuner, the last bottle of tequila, and the piggybank Hulk—again!—this time successfully, stamping out their cigarette butts on my floor, not even bothering with the window but walking in and out the front door and leaving it open behind them.

This is a true story.

This is a dream, a poem, a song, a prayer.

This is for all those trapped within the body of desire. This is for all those fleshed with the alien muscle of need.

This is for all those who would walk the avenue and say

I am sufficient in the sunlight and mercy of this day, I will have none of what you offer, no longer does my marrow ache with wanting, I crave for nothing, though I am hungry I shall hunger no more.

A Letter to James Wright

Glory of laundry aflutter from every window,
and the blessed buzz of the unseen vespa,
and the fat flies fruit-stunned in the breakfast saucers,
and the skinny street kids kicking soccer balls along the
    breakwater,
and the harborside restaurants with their neon scampi and
    sardine-packed tables,
and the sunlight and the motorboats and the colorful rowboats
    strung like ducklings amid the white yachts,
and the brash swath of the hydrofoil outbound for the islands,
Capri like a mirage on the horizon,
beautiful Ischia hidden by the headlands,
and the black bulk of Vesuvius,
and the grimy ash on the sills and balconies,
and the flowers, the bougainvillea, and the lemon tree bowers,
and the Homeric vista of dawn, mountains and islands upon
    the wine-dark sea,
and the smell of cedar and lemon,
and the taste of *prosciutto e melone*,
flesh thin as paper, sere exfoliations,
and the craft of the old man's hands as he hasps the razor
    against the haunch,
the juice and the marrow,
sugar and salt. . . .

★

This journey.

★

Naples. Saturday, May 23. Jackson is exactly six months old this morning, wriggling behind me in the baby backpack, grasping at my ears, yanking the cord of my sunglasses as if to rein in a runaway horse. In four more days it will be Sam's fifth birthday. Five years since that morning in Chicago, five years into the new geological age, the Samocene Era, the Neo-Jacksonian Epoch. Time, like the funicular, flies on tireless wings, but the three of us are hoofing it, hiking the arduous cobbled roadway of the picturesque castle in the harbor, shooting invaders from every gun-slit and portico.

What is the name of this castle?

I've misplaced the map.

*

Castel del Ovo. So named after the legendary egg said to lie hidden in a secret room within the walls; if the egg should ever break, Naples will fall.

*

Looking, from above, like white sachets or wind-whipped handkerchiefs, young brides pose on the castle causeway to be photographed in lavish wedding gowns while the police in their many-colored uniforms wave and whistle ineffectually at the free-form traffic streaming past. All the brides come here, we've been told, it's good luck, a necessary superstition. Does it have something to do with the egg?

Along with the photographers, Sam shoots them all,

infidels come to challenge his kingdom.

A beautiful afternoon, warm and breezy. Elizabeth is off with her mother and sister shopping for lace or linens or whatever it is Neapolitans do best, my body is climbing the castle with the boys but my mind is adrift among clouds and boats and poems, and it seems to me that the finest of these vessels may be "A Letter to Franz Wright." At least it is the loveliest to which I give anchorage on this day, the dearest-held poem harbored within me. There's so much I admire in it, so much to be learned—the sense of humility and awe, the wonder of its Italian landscape, its voice, its range, its texture, the charm and formal daring, the perfect pitch of its emotion, the love and respect of a father for his son.

Italy, prose poems, fathers and sons—well, obviously

I'm prejudiced.

Still I return to that work again and again, I love so many of those last poems, treasure them like sacral beings, a flowering of such magnitude near the end of a difficult life, as if the pear tree that stood for years unclothed in the rain and snow of Ohio had at the last, unbidden, blossomed.

But we are not trees and it requires an act of will for us to bloom

and it is the courage of that action I admire,

the willingness to recreate your art anew, once more, a second metamorphosis, making yours a life in the art with not merely two but three proper acts.

From the rooftop of the castle I can see it, almost, the shape of that transformation, a rebirth beneath Mediterranean skies, your own personal Italian renaissance:

the shape of a city in the shadow of a volcano

finding comfort in the arms of its bay.

★

Someone's had a reception up here. Wooden arbors of branches hung with huge ripe lemons have been tossed back into the corner, behind the cannons, with a mess of melon rinds and soggy cardboard. Lemons large and fragrant as lanterns! Last night we watched from our hotel as they projected huge slides against these upper walls to advertise an exhibition of paintings by Frida Kahlo and Diego Rivera. Some part of the castle is a museum now, though we have been unable to find it—

the room of the legendary egg, perhaps.

Jackson has dozed off, head slumped down against my shoulder, his breath tickling the hairs on the back of my neck.

Sam is wide awake and cannonading the city.

In need of fresh recruits, he scrawls urgent messages in his notebook, practicing his "own kind of writing"—a precise glyphic gibberish of squiggled letters and symbols—which I am delegated to translate into "regular writing."

We need soldiers to defend the castle. We are having a war here. You can dress up as a prince or princess. We need guys with swords and guns and cannons.

Hurry!

★

It seems an impossibly lovely touch that Franz Wright should have gone on to become a poet himself, that the burden of his father's fame has not silenced him, that the sword may in time be exchanged for the pen, creative destruction for creative aplomb. It seems too much to wish for, though I can understand how it came to pass—

I can hear it in your poem.

Such transparency, the hopes and dreams of fathers for their sons, elaborate and fragile as Fabergé eggs.

Certainly I would wish mine your courage, both kinds—the strength to persevere and the gift of change. I would wish them escape from the clutches of Ohio, whatever Ohio it is that may shadow them.

I would wish them their Italy.

*

I don't believe that Naples will ever fall. Buried in lava it would reseed itself, weeds to wildflowers to the rank and glorious verdure of this human jungle. Such a place will always, up to the last moment of the species, that final pulse of the human hive,

endure.

Sam has won the war and wants a soda.

Since we are here it will be warm and full of fizz, the straws made of paper, the coins imperial and tragic.

The stones around us testify to a thousand years of use.

From the little cafe-bar the view is a dazzle of deep blue water beyond a space of silver light and mist, burnished air, a great soaring void framed in stone, the way some people imagine the soul contained within the body, though here we approach the arena of the untellable, the wall against which the hammer shatters into shards of jewel-hard brilliance. Oblivious to us and our thirst, to the uncollected bottles and dishes of melted ice cream, to the sheer three-hundred-foot drop at his back,

oblivious to all but his stolen light

the bar boy sits in the window and leans out, headphones in his ears, tinfoil reflector held up to the sun.

The wall is still standing.

The egg has not broken.

The branch will not break.

Manitoba

Ten miles in we came upon the locusts, road striped and banded with them, fields plagued and shadowed with their mass, fulsome, darker than cloud-dapple, slick as shampoo beneath the wheels. In the next town we stopped to scrape them from the radiator with our pocket knives. Grasshoppers, their bodies crushed and mangled, scaled and armatured, primordial, pharoanic, an ancient horde of implacable charioteers, black ooze caking the headlights to blindness, mindless yellow legs still kicking. Not much in that town: sidewalks grown with goldenrod, grain elevator on the old railroad siding. Not much besides wheat and gasoline, the ragged beauty of the heat-painted prairie, wind with the texture of coiled rope, the solitude of the plains unrolling beyond limit of comprehension. It was time to hit the road. Charlie grabbed a root beer; I topped-up the oil. We hosed out the dead and drove on.

Las Vegas

1

My first time in town, passing through with Charlie, long before
the Babylonian captivity of that neon oasis, before the Hard Rock
and the Liberace Museum, the space needle Kong-a-coaster,
white tigers and mute centurions, before the hyper-
textualization of our dreams when we were yet content with
mere demesnes of poppy-colored bulbs and a cheap room at the
Prince Albert and the big cowboy waving howdy and a long night
roaming the sports books cadging tequila sunrises from zombie-
tranced keno girls amid the zero hour jangle of the slots. Blissful
oblivion. Noise and nothingness. That was all, but we loved it,
loved it completely, and when we tired of dropping slugs we did
what we always did in the places we loved: memorialized them
through the consummation of our consumerist selves, which is
to say, we bought some souvenirs.

Bolo ties and Elvis ashtrays, scorpions in lucite, lucky dice frozen
on boxcars and snake eyes.

Junk, of course, pure junk, holy junk from the sacred trove, and
we loved it wholly, unironically, with the purity of disciples, not
as kitsch but as artifacts of something splendid and inexplicable,
as we loved the textured velvet of the city itself, loved the golden
sheen of the pawn shops as we loved the old women shoveling
tokens into handbags and the hotel maids speaking Spanish at
the bus stop and the way the wind scoured the avenues as if to
render all this to Sphinxian obliquity. In the morning we saddled
up at the breakfast buffet, moved on to L.A., that crazy, long-
forgotten scene.

This was when—1981, 1982?

I have a photo of it pinned to the bulletin board: Charlie in his Schlitz beer cowboy hat beneath a globe proclaiming *World's Largest Souvenir Store* haloed by luminous, fire-streaked clouds,

Viking longboats put to the torch by sunset,

vessels cast flaming westward for Valhalla.

2

Fifteen years later I'm best man at my brother's wedding at the Silver Bells chapel on the Strip, and before the exchange of vows I hug him and hand the rings to Elvis, presiding, young and sneering, one of his less grotesque earthly manifestations, who says to the bride—my new sister-in-law—"Do you promise to love him tender, to care for his hound dog, never to step on his blue suede shoes?" At the end he sings "Viva Las Vegas" as a recessional while Sam gets up and dances in the aisle and it's all much too familiar to me from hallucinations I once was prey to concerning internment in a netherworld of go-go girls and sepulchral lights derived from the dance sequences of the very worst Elvis movies.

Clambake. Blue Hawaii. Live A Little, Love A Little.

Like a black-light painting of fluorescent gnomes, daylight drains the mystery from the city, but at night it fills back up again, a magician's trick with a glass of water. For three days we chose to see it as half-full, a fun trip for the family in its way, even with the "World of Concrete" convention in residence among us, which may or may not explain why the pall of cigarette smoke and bells and whistles induced a form of nausea that persisted even as we paraded with Sam through the pure synthetic cash-

and-carry family joy rides therein assembled, a sunny new gloss for the city of sin, a facade as misplaced as anything I can imagine, circus posters pasted across the entrance to the gas chamber, penitents come to gorge at the altar of their enslavement.

Our last morning we drove out to visit the Hoover Dam, stopping for pancakes in Boulder City before descending into the vault of that

titanic concrete angel wing

to watch vast turbines spun by weight of falling water, valves and relays riven with the electric intake and outrush, systole, diastole —

standing there and watching it, mesmerized, alive and breathing —

the many-chambered heart of a thing beyond our knowing.

Elvis Impersonators' Day, Gulfstream Park

Ansonium in the 3rd; *Lucky Dot* in the 4th; *Tiger Tilly* in the 5th.

Show time, between races, the kids climb the jungle gym while we consider the relative merits of the gyrating Elvi on stage: Billy Ray Elvis, Sirhan Elvis, Elvis E. Lee. Draught beer, tired applause. The kids pay no attention at all, though Sam knows well who Elvis is, knows him personally, from his uncle's wedding in Las Vegas; Elvis is a figure of totemic significance in Sam's world, like Godzilla or the President, uncanny but real.

Outside the paddock the horses parade manicured pathways of hibiscus like the leaders of an ancient sect fawned upon by grooms and footmen.

How else to proceed but through ritual in the presence of such lavish beasts?

So we contrive to risk our last allotted dollars in the seventh race, beguiled by omens and numerological coincidence, the chance suggestion of a sire or dame.

Along the rail the asphalt is littered with beer cups and hot-dog wrappers, stubs of lost bets Sam and his pals collect into piles, tickets to something unimaginably wonderful; seagulls squabble over pieces of popcorn and the kids chase them off among the scattered onlookers, oblivious to the last furlong of muscle thundering past.

"Sammy," Elizabeth calls after them. "Sammy, not too far!"

An old man in a porkpie hat, plaid jacket, face and hands leathered by Florida sun, a man who could be the spirit of the racetrack incarnate, turns to me and gestures with the stub of his cigar. "That's Sammy?" I nod. "You should have been here yesterday—*Sammy from Miami* paid 40 to 1 in the sixth race."

Jimmy Buffett

1

This past winter, Elizabeth, Sam, and I spent a weekend on Cabbage Key with Becky and with Larry D, our brother-in-law-to-be. They were down for a week of winter sun, escaping snowy Brooklyn, and we were overjoyed to win parole and pass a day or two at sea, and so we crossed the Everglades at dawn, north past Naples, through Fort Myers and over to Pine Island, and then a boat ride from Bokeelia with Captain Frank I. Floyd across the wide, shallow, pelican-haunted waters of Charlotte Harbor.

Southwest Florida is beautiful and terrifying, the part of America most like the frontier to me,

bulldozers idling at the gates of Eden

as nautilus-patterned retirement communities are riven from the swamplands, par 5s carved from sandy tomato fields, marinas hewn from the marl and reed beds, the shallow bays and estuarine inlets of the Mangrove Coast.

Neither God nor man has finished with this place.

2

But Cabbage Key is pretty cool. Offbeat, idiosyncratic, the Depression-era vacation home of some Midwestern industrialist, a pretty white house on a hill become a funky fisherman's hotel given over to booze and sunspot marimbas, the very place, rumor had it, whereof Jimmy Buffett wrote "Cheeseburger in Paradise," making it as well a priceless piece of Floridiana. Here in the Sunshine State, Jimmy Buffett is a sacred presence, patron saint of charter boat captains and weekend fishermen desirous of looking like charter boat captains, any white guy in a Hawaiian shirt with a sunburned nose wistful for the rum-soaked, piratical days of yore. Jimmy Buffett is our troubadour, our poet laureate, our cultural ambassador. The state tree is the cabbage palm; the state song ought to be "Margaritaville." And so, disembarking from Captain Frank's ferry ride at noon, while everyone else eats peanut butter and jelly in the room, I insist on climbing the hill to the little bar and grill to get—what else?—a cheeseburger, which tastes good, lacks fries and frills, and sets me back exactly $10.17. The price of paradise has gone up.

3

After lunch we set out in a rented skiff with an ancient Evinrude across the green bay toward Cayo Costa, the barrier island beyond which lie the deeper waters of the gulf, stopping en route to search the sandy shoals for conch shells, though most are still inhabited and we throw them back, past old abandoned houseboats tethered to trees,

flocks of heron and anhinga, hierarchies of ibis,

and then a twisting, tortuous channel through a tunnel of crab-infested mangroves, fully overgrown by their stilt-walking buttresses and trestles of roots—a maze in which I contrive to entangle my paddle, pulled inexorably from my grasp by the boat's slow momentum until it lashes back to strike my brother-in-law across the temple with a horrible smack—leading at last to a lovely green lagoon behind the fringe of white sand that fronts the gulf.

A magnificent spot.

High clouds, wide drifts of opalescent seashells, an osprey

perched on a driftwood nest tearing red hunks of flesh from a fish clenched in its talons.

Elizabeth and Becky lay out the towels. Ice from the cooler keeps Larry's eye from swelling closed. Sam runs onto the beach and says he has found a fish, a puffer fish, a lot of them, and in fact the beach is littered with the bodies of snook and grouper and yellowtail, spiny puffers, angel fish in their zebra raiment, still heaving, some of them, still beautiful, not yet bled of iridescence by the sun.

Goggle-headed, pop-eyed, abdomens burst open and protruding.

Fifty yards out, a tell-tale band of brownish water, an ochre discoloration we've learned to recognize: *Red Tide*. Sam coughs. "Why are the fish dead, Dad?" Because the water is poisoned. "Why?"

4

What can I say? The fish are killed by algae; the algae bloom in deadly numbers because they always have, though these days the Red Tide comes more often, lasts longer, due to something in the water—pollution, sewage, phosphates—who knows? Young fish are most susceptible; shellfish too absorb high quantities of neurotoxins; even we are not immune, as the algae emit a cloud of noisome spores to irritate the human respiratory system, inducing us to hack and wheeze in the salt-spray. What a downer. How unlike any song. A beach choked with ruptured fish, people coughing in a toxic wind. How unfair it seems, the somber irony of the moment, unfair to the inherent splendor of the place, unfair to Florida, unfair to Jimmy Buffett, unfair to the men roaring past us in their brilliant boats, dozens of them, hundreds, oblivious to all but the exhilaration of their pursuit. These fishermen upon the waters of the gulf, do they not see what we see? Have they averted their eyes, or is the glare just too bright? Is it our unalterable nature to be blinded to the costs of our trespass, here, amid the mangroves of paradise? I don't want the poem to end this way,

5

but how can it not?

Hours later, back on Cabbage Key, drinking—yes—margaritas, Larry's eye swollen like a prizefighter's, Sam feeding crackers to the Muscovy ducks, even then we are sun-dazzled, we see the world we choose to see, we plot a safe and familiar course among the shoals and reefs that surround us, the innumerable keys and islets of interpretation.

Jimmy Buffett wrote a song about this place.

Pirates sailed these waters once.

The Calusa lived here for two thousand years. Lacking agriculture, they ate palm nuts and prickly pears, sea turtles and sharks, subsisted on the bay's incalculable bounty of clams and oysters, scallops and conchs. That's how the hill we're sitting on was made, so curiously risen from the glass-green shallows, overgrown now with sea grape and strangler fig, buttonwood and gumbolimbo, live oak veiled in Spanish moss and the snake-like cactus that climbs the cabbage palms to hang in Medusa tresses from the fronds.

This island is composed of their discarded shells.

Capitalist Poem #42

While Elizabeth shops at Costco, Sam and I play hide & seek
among the bales and pallets in that vast warehouse of pure
    things.
Believe me, what little we do buy—napkins and pain killers,
loops of figs, loose cashews, a carton of over-ripe cantaloupes,
tubs of discount laundry detergent and the Ansel Adams desk
    calendar,
three dozen lightbulbs, twenty-two metric socket wrenches,
tinkertoys, tea bags, tennis balls, Christmas tinsel,
frozen eggrolls and midget palm trees, string cheese, soda
    crackers
and computer software—is as nothing to what we leave behind,
the merest anthill against the Great Pyramid of Cheops,
a sidewalk crevice compared to that Grand Canyon of
    commodities.
Bright laughter, summer skies. So they descend into the abyss.

A Map of Dodge County, Wisconsin

for Jane Eggert

Elk horns, beaver teeth, bell jars, bauxite; cap pistols, pin cushions, air rifles, sacks of dice; pewter doves and tin lovebirds, plaster polar bears and ceramic moose; potato mashers, rolling pins, canning jars, ladles; rococo salvers and baroque cornucopias; shoe trees, cheese wheels, antique beakers of Lash's bitters; margarita glasses stolen from Chi-Chi's; Olde Copenhagen candy bowls in cyanine, verbena, sienna, and spruce; salt and pepper shakers shaped like Li'l Black Sambo; a Queen Victoria tea service and the Joan Baez songbook; geodesic ashtrays from the New York World's Fair; a smiling Air India kewpie panjandrum; a Bob Johnson hand-carved "Bluebill Drake"; an *Atlas of Norse Myth and Icelandic Sagas*; a guide to Wisconsin's favorite trade in the souvenir taps and banners and trays from Hamm's and Pabst and Miller and Blatz; a map of Dodge County in the vintage collections of brown glass bottles embossed with the totem and heraldic crests of the local burghers' vanished brews: White Cap, North Star, Gold Label, Falls City; Zeigler's, Kurth's, Grat's, Jung's; Alps Brau and Fox DeLuxe, Holiday and Munchner; Hauenstein, Pioneer, Chief Oshkosh, Oconto.

Four Clouds Like the Irish in Memory

First memory of school: sitting in the grass beneath a blossoming dogwood tree while the teacher explains how to write a poem.

Boisterous sun, orbital crab apples, isn't the springtime beautiful? What do the clouds look like? Butterfly, banana split, polar bear, clown. What does the dogwood look like, its bracts and tiers and white cascades of flowers? Snowflakes. A birthday cake. Good, good. Like going to New York for the holidays, like heaven or the George Washington Bridge at night, its titanium spans and whirligigs, garlands of popcorn, garlands of cranberries, baked ham and my grandfather's accordion, my mother and her sisters trying out their old Shirley Temple routines amidst an Irish stew of relatives and well-wishers immersed for the day in the nostalgic mist and manners of the old sod.

Shamrock, whiskey bottle, subway train, diaspora.

One year my grandfather drove with us back to Washington after Christmas. I remember him chiefly for that matchless accordion, the hats and boats he made from newspaper, the senility that claimed him like an early snowfall—

as I remember my father's father for the crafty wooden puzzles he assembled at the kitchen table with a box of Ritz crackers and a quart of Rheingold beer—

but this was my mother's father, a countryman from Donegal, famous for long strolls in Riverside Park collecting weeds for home remedies, for walking the bridge to save a penny on a pack of cigarettes. He worked forty years as a ticket taker in the subway, pent too long 'mid cloisters dim, and somewhere in southern New Jersey, in the backseat of the station wagon looking out past the turnpike traffic, he said, in his thick brogue, to no one in particular, *goodness,*

I had no idea there were such great forests left.

Tabernacle, New Jersey

is not the place I thought it was. All these years, crossing the dwarf-pine coastal midlands, the map of New Jersey gone AWOL from the road atlas, what I'd remembered as Tabernacle was actually Chatsworth, two old colonial towns, ten miles apart, peas in a pod, nothing could be more similar and nothing could be more distinct. Chatsworth, I guess, was named by the homesick for a town left behind in England, while Tabernacle implies not only a house of worship but a sanctuary and a shelter, a dwelling place and a covenant, an immaculate coal in the hearth of the New World, invested today in exurban restoration, garden centers and antique marts, new subdivisions in the old peach orchards, the historic church signed and posted for day-trippers out from Philadelphia. Tabernacle is a sign of things to come while Chatsworth is purely a thing of the past, a place so momentary its passage is forgotten even before its official contemplation—was that it?—ramshackle houses set back beneath shade trees, front porches sagged and winded, a poster for the annual BBQ & turkey shoot at the Antler Hall, a roadhouse and general store at the crossroads of the Pine Barrens, that comical backwater of forgotten towns, Batsto and Ong's Hat, Leektown and Double Trouble, so named when muskrats gnawed through the town dam two times in a single month. Muskrats. Twice.

What I like about Chatsworth is its sandy transience, its ageless and indelibly American dereliction. People came to Chatsworth, lived for awhile, and moved on. They settled down, hunted deer, kilned bricks, scrounged the deposits of pig iron from the soil, harvested the cranberry bogs, chopped down the pine trees and burned them for charcoal, raised up kids for a generation or two, then headed out for greener pastures, taking Chatsworth with them and leaving Chatsworth behind. A town like Chatsworth would be right at home among tired Tidewater tobacco fields or the chicken houses of the Eastern Shore, along the old wagon roads at some ford of the Potomac, the Susquehanna, the Delaware, the James, anywhere at all in the majestic and underappreciated Mid-Atlantic region, which is home to me, central and definitive, though for that matter you could find Chatsworth in most of Appalachia and scattered throughout the South, and into the riverine Midwest, Ohio to Iowa, and so into the plains, and across the mountains to the apple orchards of Oregon, and even in the altogether unnatural badlands of Utah where, once, lonely to the point of desperation, I passed through just such a place on a Sunday afternoon when the Volunteer Fireman's Picnic was in progress, a group of families eating hot dogs and buttered corn, some kids with red and yellow balloons, people waving in kindly invitation as I slowed to a crawl, and thought about stopping, and drove on.

Listen, I've driven all over this country, I've spun the odometers of a dozen bad cars, I don't know how many road atlases I've worn to sacrificial shreds, but in each and every one New Jersey opens like a flower, dead center, stapled twice through the heart. Thus it is median and first to weaken. Until one sad and inevitable day the Garden State disappears forever, blossom of weary abandonment. Which is why for all these years I mistook Chatsworth for Tabernacle, driving blind across the heart of the state to our cherished summer weeks at the shore, stopping for tomatoes at the Green Top Market, for frozen yogurt at the Dairy Bar in Red Lion, steered by memory from landmark to landmark along 206 or 70, 532 or 563, it hardly matters which road you take, it hardly matters the number or the sign, even without a map I can find it, nameless or mistaken, end or beginning, north or south or east or west, because Chatsworth is everywhere and Chatsworth is everything: dwelling place, covenant, congregation, tabernacle.

The Wreck

Again on the highway with tears in my eyes, cadenced by rhythm of concrete and steel, music of cloud vapor, music of signs— Blue Flame Clown Rental/Color Wheel Fencing—again overcome, again fever-driven, transported among the pylons and skid marks of the inevitable, sirens and call boxes of a life I have laid claim to with a ticket found by chance in the pocket of a secondhand overcoat. And if it should come to that, if my fate is to be splayed on an altar of steel, heart held forth on an Aztec dagger of chrome, if this, then still I say it was beautiful, the freedom and speed with which you conveyed me, the way and the will, and I won't renounce the reek of acrid rubber or deny the need that sent me there, and I will not regret the purpose, the vehicle, the white line, the choice, and I will not mistake the message for the voice.

Campbell McGrath

Thumbing the road atlas, I imagine that ultimate voyage,
transcontinental, multinational, taken the long way on the
     diagonal,
Florida to Alaska, because there are many Campbells
but only one McGrath, and it is there, arrow in the heart of the
     wilderness
beyond Denali, beyond the cold waters of the Kuskokwim
     where
the last and farthest roads give way to ruts and tracks
across the tundra, snow and distance, a vastness, an emptiness,
     neverending.
Unfathomable road trip. Frigid, Stygian destination.
And a beginning, here and now, raveled twine humid and
     umbilical,
point of embarkation for the labyrinth of the nominal,
here and now, in hot and floral Campbell, Florida,
west of Kissimmee, south of Orlando, then north to encounter
the next most proximal, cleaving the concave condo banana
and the Marshes of Glynn across Georgia to Savannah,
and through the piney woods of Caroline, 77 all the way to
     Wytheville,
then into the deepest darkest of the wild and wonderful,
West Virginia, country roads and toothless ancients, carry me
     home
to Appalachia, and a trestle over the river to Campbell, Ohio,
subsumed by Youngstown, cold-rolled corridor of slag,
now west and south, up, up and away, rust and ash supplanted
by bluegrass, and across the Mississippi at Finley to Campbell,
     Missouri,

earthworm spoonhandled in the arms of the flooded muddy,
not far from Braggadocio, Currentview, or Hayti,
then southwest through Pocahontas, Campbell Station and
    Arkedelphia,
Arkansas, bound for the land of Matador and Lone Star,
asphalt beeline direct for Campbell, kin to Commerce,
colossus astraddle Route 66, midway betwixt Dallas and Paris,
then drive all day to get out of Texas, arid and blameless,
    enough said
about that sadness, Roswell, Flagstaff, even Las Vegas,
bitter coagulant blood from a stone, into the vale of borax and
    bone
and up the east slope of the Sierra Nevada and down
again through the ghost towns of gold country,
north of Yosemite, down to the boundless oasis of the valley,
silver aqueduct of dreams and fertility, south through Lodi,
stemming the grapevine from Patterson to San Jose,
shadow of the Bay and silicon suburbia, sweet sweet Campbell,
    California,
last of the first on that golden coast, that homonymic host,
lest we forget a slew of sibling claimants, various and variant,
Campbellsport, Wisconsin, Campbellsville and
    Campbellsburg, Kentucky,
and Campbellsburg, Indiana, sister city settled by emigrants
in a meadow of yarrow and horse-high hay,
and fields of rusted cars outside Campbellstown, PA,
and not just townships and municipalities but even the
    counties,
as again in Kentucky, heart of the mighty Campbell country,
and north again, further north, across the border and all over
    Canada,
Campbellston, Campbellford, Campbellbay,
the great Campbell River, on Vancouver Island,

whence carted by orcas across the black waters
and back to the mainland at Bella Coolla, British Columbia,
and up the oily scrim of the Alcan through Vanderhoof and
    Hazleton,
White Horse where the boom once was, and into Alaska
to complete the equation, cruising the blacktop on moosewatch
    to Fairbanks,
a road of summer gravel through Chatanika to Eureka,
along the Tanana, and the vast ice artery of the heartless Yukon,
by ferry to a hardscrabble roadhead of washboard near Ruby,
through Long down to Poorman, wary animals in the alder
    scrub
and smell of rancid chicken blood and vague directions south,
into the emptiness, toward the headwaters of the primitive
    Nowitna,
permafrost spun to mud along the last miles of navigable
    tirehold,
thickets of brush and intractable scree, chill of dusk in the
    embers' lees,
constellated ashes, glacial till, light in the distance could be
    foxfire
or sign of an early aurora, skirl of tundra and guessed-at ranges,
snow dragging with it the whiteness of the interior,
white quadrants of impersonal destiny, beyond any known
    boundary
of the geological survey, where the atlas surrenders its horn of
    hooded inklings
and mute words are limned in the halo-glimmer of the
    nameless,
and the dogs howl in their traces, and the sled path disintegrates
to chalk-track ellipses. . . . All maps are useless now.
These final steps must be taken alone, like the ragged first
    footfalls

of some yolk and caul hatchling along a wild river,
in the woods, at the foot of the mountains, in a valley of stars,
beyond vehicle of the familiar, language or skin,
in the darkness without and the darkness within.
There, where the road ends, the real journey begins.

About the Author

CAMPBELL MCGRATH is the author of three previous full-length collections: *Capitalism, American Noise,* and *Spring Comes to Chicago.* His recent awards include the Kingsley Tufts Prize, the Cohen Prize, a Guggenheim Fellowship, and a Witter-Bynner Fellowship from the Library of Congress in association with the Poet Laureate. McGrath teaches creative writing at Florida International University and lives in Miami Beach with his wife and two sons.